A History of the Only War

Dear David and other editors:

Thanks for publishing "Speech" and "Torch Song" first in Court Green, the second issue of which is just as exciting as the first!

Chris
10/20/05

Also by Christopher Davis

The Tyrant of the Past and the Slave of the Future

The Patriot

A History of the Only War

poems

Christopher Davis

Four Way Books
New York City

Distributed by
University Press of New England
Hanover and London

Editorial Office
Four Way Books
POB 535, Village Station
New York, NY 10014
www.fourwaybooks.com

Library of Congress Catalogue Card Number: 2004101055

ISBN 1-884800-66-1

Cover art: Brian Rumbolo

Cover design by Pablo A. Medina for Cubanica

This book is manufactured in the United States of America and
printed on acid-free paper.

Four Way Books is a not-for-profit organization. We are grateful
for the assistance we receive from individual donors, foundations,
and government arts agencies.

Distributed by University Press of New England
One Court Street, Lebanon, NH 03766

ACKNOWLEDGMENTS
These poems first appeared in the following journals:

Agni Review: "Abroad"

American Literary Review: "A Real World Arrogates Self-Love,"
    "At Saint-Martin-in-the-Fields"

American Poetry Review: "Greedy for Less," "The Matter"

Bellingham Review: "You, Lonesome American,"
    "Tchaikovsky as the Water of Winter"

Black Warrior Review: "Nod," "What We Left in San Francisco"

Boston Book Review: "Sangre de Cristo," "Pietà"

Colorado Review: "On the Soul's Immortality"

Controlled Burn: "The Knower of the Field," "Two Romances"

Court Green: "Speech," "Torch Song"

Denver Quarterly: "The Pseudo-Homosexual," "The Village Idiot
    Inside His Hide," "The Village Idiot's Offensive,"
    "Some Feeling," "Sunlight As Sword," "Teenage Waste Land"

Field: "Under the Projection Booth," "Sustenance," "Incest,"
    "A History of the Only War"

Fence: "Prayer for Reunification"

Five A.M.: "In the Intake Center"

Harvard Review: "The Village Idiot as Stopped Buck"

Interim: "Why Not Pleasure the Bigot's Body,"
    "Homotets and Faggotelles"

The Journal: "Love," "Trade"

Jubilat: "Our Pursuit of Happiness"

Lit: "The Pederast as Pedagogue"

Massachusetts Review: "Trying Not to Drown Out One's Own
    Voice," "Her Renaissance"

North Carolina Literary Review: "Political Sonata"

Ohio Review: "Echo Homo"

Passages North: "Requiem"

Pequod: "From the Wilderness of Stars,"
    "Without External Reference"

Prairie Schooner: "The Village Idiot During The Reconstruction,"
    "To the Village Idiot Inside Our Haunted House"

Quarterly West: "The Art of War"

Solo: "His Company Thrown Open to the Public"

Sonora Review: "A Symbolic Sense of Self,"
    "Minimus, to Himself"

Sundog: "Two Closet Cases"

Volt: "Owed"

Some of these poems appeared in the ezines *Shampoo*, *canwehaveourballback* and *Electronic Poetry Review*.

The following poems appear in *Word of Mouth: An Anthology of Gay American Poetry*, edited by Timothy Liu, Talisman House, 2000: "Sangre de Cristo," "The Knower of the Field," "The Pseudo-Homosexual," "Why Not Pleasure the Bigot's Body," and "Nod."

"Nod" appears in *American Poetry: The Next Generation*, edited by Gerald Costanzo and Jim Daniels, Carnegie Mellon University Press, 2000, and in *American Diaspora*, edited by Virgil Suarez and Ryan G. Van Cleave, University of Iowa Press, 2001.

"Pietà" appears in *Vespers: Religion and Spirituality in Twenty-First Century America*, edited by Virgil Suarez and Ryan G. Van Cleave, University of Iowa Press, 2003.

"Displaced Person" appears in *Red, White, and Blues: Poets on the Promise of America*, edited by Virgil Suarez and Ryan G. Van Cleave, University of Iowa Press, 2004.

Thanks to the MacDowell Colony for a helpful residency.

This book is dedicated to my mother,
Coleen Mae Cockerill Davis, 1930-2000.

Coriolanus: Let them hang!
Volumnia: Ay, and burn too.

CONTENTS

III: INSIDE

SPEECH

The monster is here, my friend.
This private voice. This ugly sculpture
plopped on thee.

Naturally
predatory,
imaginary,

clothed all in white,
a dogwood petal, an ejaculation,
I'm a germ.

I do interiors in mismatched, random greens,
the emerald sofa a wave growing in a bay,
the easy chair a grassy mound, a grave.

I'm some body buried
in beige slacks, a coat
of crust-brown suede:

a toasted hunk
censors should choke
on to start each day.

I'll try talking with you perfect, no, poetic,
working to promote the guileless stutter,
public pain fucks can't dismantle yet.

I shall leave
endless messages
on each machine.

I

OUTSIDE

NOD

In this mind
beyond dry cornstalks
I come across
my patriarch's abandoned Cadillac

the door gapes
I crawl in
try turning the wheel
it does turn

I tease the radio's knob
twiddling it between pointer and thumb
clicking it on off
clicking it on off

turning it up all the way
hearing nothing
taking in the pain
singing in the pain

Enough. Enough. We interrupt this whining
to broadcast more cowboy yodeling,
the starting of your engines,
gentlemen.

Who'd jump this old thang?
Poisonous pokeweed prods through the bumper.
Why not kiss its dents, fate's public sculpture?
Let it rust out here a few more days.

It might yet get us
where we need to go
if there's no solid place to go
no world called home

TRYING NOT TO DROWN OUT ONE'S OWN VOICE

My songwriter pal and I
had a plan to flee America,
to tour Europe as a dynamic duo,
me a punk Garfunkel sort of standing
up there, trying not to squeak, bellow.
"When you sing along with the radio,
stick with the range you pick first,"
he advised. "Just listen to yourself
and make it work."

"My life got easier," the professor
of the avant-garde whispered,
"when a lover mumbled that our mumbles
and our silences express what's going on
inside us, what we're feeling, even more
than our words do." She hated me
when I confessed
I'd had my loud cat gassed.

"*Lindo*, when you don't know what to say
don't say a thing," chuckled the guy
who'd begged to fuck me all summer.
The rubber broke, he mentioned
he was sick, and then he swore
I'd gained a partner forever.

Outside an Oxford bus station,
drunk since my plane had taken off,
the coach trip from Heathrow a blur behind me,
I overheard an upright wino warn his colleague,
sprawled out on the sun-soaked sidewalk,
"Get up, sir! Stop being so self-
assured!"

ON THE SOUL'S IMMORTALITY

1.
Giggling, weeping, trying
to feel someone else's
pain, I wrapped

a first aid sack from the Great War,
its white cotton spackled with brown
flecks, the blood of frightened boys, around
a frightened kitten's head.

Inside that womb, pieces
of black oilcloth, what the French farmers used
in place of blown-out panes.

Wouldn't it feel nice to live
beyond control, the mind
responsible, responsive?

I'm the kind of jerk who,
jerking off in my apart-
ment, locks the bathroom door,

the walls all
mirrored, countless re-
productions of me doing me re-

ceding around me
forever.

Hear the laughter
of my inner curator?

He would rather
watch me read:

Food in History
Sex in History
The Dawn of Man

2.
Hear that click-clack of hooves?
Out there, in the graveyard,
a buck, its antlers many-
tipped, glances back
as if wanting us,
reader, nearer,
its hips sway-
ing as it tip-
toes away

into the evergreen shrubs
around the dumpster.

THE PSEUDO-HOMOSEXUAL

Hopkins had to glance away from pretty boys.
He felt safe, loving untouchables.
Moses marched down with the Word
and glared at men in make-up worshiping
the touchy-feely image.
At the Young Men's Christian Association
gym, *anyone* might freak
out,
trying to see butterflies turn into buffy bunnies,
trying to avoid their glassy glances
down
at the dumbbell rolling closer
to one's tongue.
If others make us
into positivists, can't
the shattering of all relationships
be called transcendence?
Why not toss off love,
ejaculate loudly into a squad car?
From the salad bar, I took a hunk of tuna.
In my kitchen, I set it down upon
the stomach-pink floor tiles: the fat lad deep inside me,
my sad past's inner child
whom I hate, intend to get,
scuttled out from under the icebox,
nibbled at that offering
like two men gnawing
at each other's flinching
faces. Under
my back porch,
a black bitch twists,
starving for the milk
you
have to put out, fucker,
more than once.

HIS COMPANY THROWN OPEN TO THE PUBLIC

1.
One who knows our shit stinks prays
in a pew. Its hard back hurts his back.

His dead boyfriend's dry come glitters
on the comforter he presses to his cheek.

2.
He bows his head
as if his flesh
were a teardrop, surrender

welling through his nervous system's
web of feeling our fingers could tickle,
pop, pointing

out a consciousness
which is contentless,
conscienceless,

a blaze of abstraction he actually saw
once, sunset hitting a rearview mirror,
an explosion in a desert.

His eyes, each one the weight
of a collapsing star, withdrew
to hide among his privates.

3.
If he were infected, would he glare
into our singing faces
or hide his eyes behind his hand,
seeing no evil, no good?

12

Would he squat
under an exit sign
and listen to our singing,
happy to be breathing?

He might feel sort of pointlessly humane,
forgiving everybody who hurt him,
our smiles shining not far away
from his flinching face.

SANGRE DE CRISTO

An aging intellectual collected evergreens
in the green gravel of his art museum's back yard.
Did he want my love? "The force
of my own personality has always

seemed enough for me," he whispered,
screaming when I crowned his big
bronze statue of a stallion
with my tear-soaked Speedos.

I rode alone through twinkling dust,
loving the sunset, crooning anthems
to a brand new herd of bison
minting silhouettes across the cash-green grass...

crossing the bridge, I bowed out
over curled-in ram horn handlebars,
admiring my fat shadow hugging
the freshet's
        surface, its quick-
                silver glass glints...

in an abandoned Penitente morada,
its adobe walls like melting flesh,
I prayed, With all this beauty all
around us, does it matter if one hardens?

Comes again? That last late night,
a black pit bull yapped into our bedroom.
Drunk on Irish whiskey, he hollered,
"Holy hell! A hedgehog! At last!"

His nightmare was absolutely suicidal.

Red peppers dangled
from the eave of a gazebo
in which an orchestra of soldiers
droned golden oldies,

a shirtless fighter pilot waking up, humming

in damp clover.

TRADE

1.
This kid, in a convenience store, frowned on my fly, fingers moving
under his zipper. I tried hardening my character. He seemed so thin.

Perched cross-legged on the love hotel bed, he looks
very thin. *Money* he says. So it's a trap. *I'm broke*

I say, offering up half of what the room cost.
He just stares at my bill in the air. Pouting,

whispering something about rice, he shows
his empty wallet. So he's a hungry whore.

Behind his head, beyond the window,
a neon crucifix flickers, shorting out.

2.
In a landscape architect's pickup,
workers squat around a succulent,

their uniforms the same green as the elephant-ear leaves
hiding their hands. Twilight smells of rambutan, durian,

that acrid-sweet perfume. I'll buy each boy a soft drink,
green, cold, as sweet as it could be, my fingers fondling

their harps, their humming, nervous ribcages, tracing
on a notebook page the outline of my left hand, tips

of the forefinger and thumb joined, gesturing
okay, the feeling body showing, never telling.

MINIMUS, TO HIMSELF

In her white plastic chair, the postmodern critic, hunched
over a meat-pink wedge of watermelon pressed against

her lips, scowls your way like some rough beast.
Swallow black seeds, you need to scream.

Lifting weights, you tend to gaze
at your mind's two-way mirror:

in this inner art museum, your image quivers,
leaning, staring into an oil forest, his nude

knees rubbed
by the soft velvet rope,

his trembling finger touching
glass: he can't

impress his print, his sworl
of oil, upon bark.

Your eyes scan the dry boards of the porch, counting
ants scampering over paper clips, multicolored, scattered.

Wind chimes tinkle near your ear, making
mote-stuffed air around you laugh, laugh.

That friendly curator is on his way,
bringing all the armfuls of day lilies

he's been picking. He loves to stop
to kneel in icy waterfalls, and sing.

YOU, LONESOME AMERICAN

Sniff the radiator,
lick the silver bird
glued to a Ford's hood

by some owner,
not the maker.
It molders,

this pickup's brown
rust-spotted chassis
sinking in red mud,

its bed, half-filled
with rainwater, offering
a mirror to the hot sky.

Its windshield's blown,
door window burst,
the rearview

wrenched down,
facing ripped
impressions

in the fake hide pew,
the stick shift bent
into a question mark,

the radio tugged out
of the charred dash,
its red grounding wire

curling, cut off,
from a black hole.
A radio meant pleasure,

hopeless hymns
our only chance
to torch loud love.

HOMOTETS AND FAGGOTELLES

1. *Against a Tree*

This is a lovely place. The music, mostly: quick
hisses, tires, radio through rolled-down window,

drunk teens shouting some greatest hit,
a guy playing guitar in the park hot but

not necessarily bothered beneath white
wife beater rhyming with full moon.

"Feels like the First Time." He
has as much right to life as I,

excluded from people, un-
doing my fuchsia blouse,

loving him not,
loving him not.

2. *The Personal is Political?*

Wouldn't that take a performer,
his habitat his hammerklavier?

Always travel with a choirboy,
your identical twin. In motels,

force him to "do it," pledge
allegiance to the fag, seize

the gay, pray
them anthems.

TEENAGE WASTE LAND

Side One

Mother, with child, ate nothing
but Froot Loops for nine months.

When she whined,
"The last time

we fucked, you had just
dug *Making Love*,"

father, Rhett Butler, clenched her skull
and tried to crush it like a nut.

Father never
"had a cow"

as the lyric I, learning to manipulate
his stick shift, failed.

Side Two

Setting this ass upon the fountain's curved
edge, my spent breath brittle, frigid, around

these clenched fists, I just bought an awful record,
screeching film score music from *My Struggle*.

That's dough I could easily have blown
on a burst, inside my mouth, of pleasure.

Fog gasses the junipers
arranged in a straight line.

Around my boots, flappers flip-
flop, battle for the heap's top,

for my spilled seed,
not a perfume squirt.

ECHO HOMO

Last night, at my behest, a catamite
did batten upon my body, curled,
laughing, against his warm ribs.

That beautiful blond stripper
had a black Prussian eagle
tattooed on his inner thigh.

A dot of the white death
plopped on my eyeball.
Alone at last, I trembled.

Sucking my thumb,
I felt the bone,
the nail a shield

against this tongue.
The less said,
the better,

I reckon.
Normal, Illinois.
Starkville, Mississippi.

In the morning, attacking
my flesh voice, I sliced my Adam's apple,
the red dot on my white collar a kamikaze flag.

WHY NOT PLEASURE THE BIGOT'S BODY

The beautiful black boy, thin and strong, his abs world class,
swivels
toward me, then
away.

He leaps, he's on his knees, he stretches himself flat across the
        stage, his tongue
twisting: he needs

anyone at all to stick
into his tighty whities
one damn dollar bill.

Pushed up against
the mirror wall,
he torques his torso, and watches

the white irises rise
into his eyes—
afraid to peek out into our faces?

My buddy believes he's defensive: "Why
can't he make eye contact?" Obviously, he can
feel

all around him our disgust: a fat
fuck just announced he don't
do chocolate.

Let me tell you,
I like my black guys
hung, not hanged.

Imagine that little nigger
dragging me into his bedroom,
allowing me to bow into his lap.

He'd fling me away,
his baby girl shrieking,
ignored, in her bedroom.

We split Illusions.
Marching across the parking lot,
I pick up a dead limb, shake it

at two buzzards circling on high,
cruising a pickup, an old troll waiting
to be picked up, maybe

loved. Waiting. Waiting.
Always caught in traffic.
Just let them try.

TWO ANTHEMS

1. *Anonymity*

Loudspeakers wooed us, cross over, enter
cardboard farms, listen, bulls groan, getting

milked, pagans, natives, grasp at soft white
palms, harvest pennies, try second-guessing

where, in this glee club, one stands, how
each saves his own damn place, finally.

2. *Alienation*

Elsewhere, jets exploded in silhouettes, a galaxy
of headlights shining on this down-to-earth body

buying quiet, normal still lives, bursting purple figs.
In dull developments, bright knives. If one could see

the cannonball approaching, one could feel sure of losing
head. A meadow a mile from battle would have sounded

silent. Tonight, I'll hide, inside the mind, the I
high in the violin, giggling, frightened, crying.

PRAYER FOR REUNIFICATION

Our invert needed to be thought unique.
Besieged by black-haired heads in Seoul's subway,
he clamped on his headphones to hear their tunes.
"How group-centered they are!" he thought. "I hate
these nicey-nice political love hymns."

He slapped in his Sinatra tape, and hummed.
He flinched when Frank crooned, of the lady tramp,
"She'd never bother with people she hates."
He gazed at the soldiers, their cheekbones, mouths.
He yearned to hear, "Yankee go home...with me!"

Did they think him a whore-raping GI
from the fifties? Horny and sad, he sussed
out the terrain. The twinkling glass lenses
over their eyes fired at his conscience,
that gauze across his inward-bent desire.

Near midnight curfew, blitzed boys, arms wrapped fast
around each other's necks, roared, as one god,
"The March of Im," about a hero killed
by riot cops; when the train swayed, they puked
all over each other, and laughed, hurting

our lonesome loser's left-out feelings worse.
He thought, "If, like MacArthur, I divide
the group, marching between two boys as if
on a blitzkrieg from Inchon to Pusan,
destroying support systems, wrecking all

communication, I can turn toward one,
at least, capture a chance, if not a kiss,
and win, perhaps, deep down inside myself,
the split-up of my folks, that two-headed
dragon, the black head my morose father's,

the red, spewing wine burning like napalm,
my desperate mother's. This monster shrieks
inside my ears. It bites my mind, trying
to chew itself apart, but it begs me
to drop a blade through it, hew it in half."

The subway train swayed like a dragon's tail
around a curve, snapping his body back
against a black tuxedo, forward, smack,
into a red *hanbok*, that puffy silk
wedding dress hiding the bride's tits and ass.

Before his eyes, the two doors opened wide.
The train gulped schools of party animals
smelling like fish. A baby's ugly head,
bald as a monk's, got pushed against his heart.
The fish-shaped eyes gazed up into his globe.

Did they fear sky-blue irises above
cheeks of pink sand, a beached beast's gaping mouth
roaring queer baby talk? Inchon was ours.
The baby burst. Its mother moaned and swayed,
smiling, trying to mute it with her love.

Lost in a demonstration of black hair,
the crisscrossed arms of boys, his mouth beside
faces bursting with song, glasses one tear,
a drum of love pounding inside his ribs,
our hero rubbed his loins into a spine,

his orgasm feeling useless, a prayer,
his whole body wrapped in white fluorescence,
the receiving center, exfoliating,
invisible, essential, of our world
on which, thank God, the Bomb was not dropped thrice.

THE ART OF WAR

In a tube stop, a busker
plucks notes, singular
and slow, from his sitar.

A banker untucks his blouse,
extends both arms, white wings,
and dances, slowly, swaying in,

out, his head
nodding, his eyes
closing, his brain

aimed in against
his face, his lover
lost

behind commuters;
inside instrument-
shaped strangers,

nervous endings
seem to him
to jittle,

little notes
like glass and nails
from fate's exploding train.

THE KNOWER OF THE FIELD

Horny, tired, stumbling
down Phuket ("fuckit"?) Beach,
I suppose one can only think
about that vision of white light
I came to Asia praying
I might have. Evening burns.
The wet beach glimmers, golden.
My torso's shadow buries
this dropped coconut, split
open. I step back:
the silhouette of my bust's filled
with both the halves, as if
the brown shell were my broken
skull, the white meat, freckled
with pink sand, my exposed
brain. A boy toy watches me.
He wears nothing but cut-offs,
his hooking fingers hanged
through his belt loops.
He tiptoes closer, asks, am I
married? I nod, lying.
I glance down at his fly.
"I go back to your room."
"No," I mumble, "I can't pay
for sex." I walk away.
Just past the surf's reach,
in white, dry sand, children
built a castle of wet sand,
its keep surrounded by high
crenellated walls. Between
the beach and street, in evergreens,
the locusts scream. Another sky-
scraping hotel's under construction,
its metal skeleton erect
behind the tee-shirt shacks,

the grind and crunch of dragging
chains hurting my brain, the boy
behind me, suddenly, sobbing,
"I go your room, I have no cash,
I need to eat." "I'm sorry, I can't
give you money to make love."
My red legs throb. I feel
surrounded by the world's heat rising
from this sand like powdered bone.
The body, or the trying
to get into it
and out of it
at the same time
right now seems
the root of all
madness.

II

AGAINST

LOVE

Lacking all vocabulary
for softness, democracy,

these wide shoulders trembling
winglessly, this jerk offering

up this fistful of daisies, little
white stallions, bone corral:

one life's bright sentence,
a coming heaven's essence.

&

In a theater of language, jacking
off self, I saw white noise rising.

Laugh that that were laundry,
air around us both a boundary

stuffed with stinks, Hamburger
Helper, patchouli, weed killer,

shadows of phone lines criss-
crossing those leafless twigs.

PIETÀ

A mother and her son tug
up out of the dumpster
a mirror, body-
length, un-
broken.

Bowing, he thrusts his closed eyes into his mom's floral blouse.
He sniffs the gardenia-scented shampoo in the gray curls of her hair;
he adores their sweet fragility, so soft against his cheek.

On a peach-colored late spring afternoon,
in his queen-sized bed, he bent
into a question mark, and beat off,
for the first time, his attacker,
planting, in his navel, the seeds
of a sex addict's future, banging

on the locked green door of the condemned bath house,
weeping as the bus split, minus one, for the orgy,
him hunched over a porn periodical, feeling
some hot stranger's glance pass
over him,

away,
the dark night of his dong a summer day.

Mother, may one
come inside the air, its butterflies
fluttering around a hummingbird?

Coyotes whine, their voices
infantile, effeminate, like
the cries of mothers and their babies
shoved, for heaven's sake, into the ovens.

POLITICAL SONATA

Last night, I stumbled into a coffee house.
On the stage, a woman squatted, her white hair
like wind-torn cumulus, her eyes
closed, her legs crossed under her muumuu.
She'd just asked her voyeurs to breathe deeply,
open their heart chakras, teach the world to sing.
Then she recited. Each line had love and space
and God as She. She called her poems prayers.
She kneaded hair-wisps this way, that way,
like Einstein. That gentle smile. Outside,
in the bars and alleys, the sexiest of guys,
dark-haired and smelling sweet, ripped off
their admirers, especially those soft boys
whom they liked. A waitress gave a Christian
too much cash back, making change, but who
said anything? I liked the poet, even though
her work revealed perfection of the life.
She helped me feel weaker than I am,
or ever can be. I needed to be perched
upon your knee, my friend, feeling
the awkwardness of two bodies,
neither of us symbols, both of us mortals,
your lips inside my ear shell
whispering the sound of surf
as on the rain-wet street the tires
of passing hearses softly sobbed.

GREEDY FOR LESS

Everybody singing,
standing, sinking, un-
touchable, uncertain,

afraid of air, feeling
something nobody
feels, palms open,

eyes, dyed green
through stained
glass, drawn

more to beauty than to logic,
those two wreaths nooses of laurel
around the gnawed neck of a cross:

inside this skull, disgust.
That's what the soul has.
That's why a baby cries.

TWO CLOSET CASES

1. *Bruce*

His solid gold wedding band rests
upon a brown leaf in the pattern
of the Comfort Inn bedspread.

A print of some fall copse,
complete with mending wall,
hangs over his Roman head.

His vague cologne smells like an ad:
imagine our hero laughing, kissing
his woman in the sea spray,

his white blouse blown open, torso
like shining armor. His steady
palm slides down from his chest

to his crotch. He wants me
to make him a job offer. Old
trolls mumble inside this mind

in silence: "We're all products.
He can't love a sad man's tears.
You'll never overhear his fears."

2. *Mark*

On an April night, my friend's eyes seem dark,
all the handsome men in him he could become
cowering behind his irises, their shields.

Against my lips, the round rim
of the beer bottle feels so cold,
a dead child's kiss.

He peeks at my heart.
I want to close my eyes,
to feel more like a symbol.

"Your bedroom door," he whispers,
"looks like a tomb entrance. I'm looking
for broad feelings." Above the intersection,

a stop light throbs, tinting tips of leaves
as if they had been dipped in a wound,
that red blur on the wet asphalt.

This hand grabs the rock inside his pants.
Lashed to a dogwood, a pit bull pants,
too happy, actually, to spring, to attack.

OWED

Trembling at the edges of riots, great
queens prayed, "O my people, tug

my calm compassion out through
this berlin's gilt window frame.

Bend it back in as frightened empathy.
Do I feel helpless not unlike a subject?

Kids, reach in, snatch my crown.
I'll chase you around, my nibbled

nails stretched over your heads,
mud flying up into my robes.

Let this solid flesh feel too,
too awkward, unprotected.

Go, dump red poster paint
into each intersection. Let

tread prints criss-
cross, inscribing,

all over town, the tired
lines in our eyes. Just

to make love just
to feel on top."

IN THE INTAKE CENTER

Pulled over, I thought, "No one
ought to drink and drive.
If I'm drunk, I need

penalization.
And anger absolutely
never helps a fucking thing."

Odd, this passive feeling,
curiosity, acceptance,
in authority's embrace.

"Defend the law as you would the city walls,"
said Heraclitus. Socrates died
rather than hurt the law.

According to Cicero,
the strongest friendship
must be destroyed

if it takes break-
ing the law
to keep it.

I hate
how mom, lonesome fag hag, avoids
paying bills, my love electric

with resentment.
She buys, she eats, an effaced beast,
the tender media her only friends.

Yesterday,
a social worker, a soft male,
sensitive, judgmental, forgiving,

described attachment dis-
order, deprived delinquents
going with the flow.

Her pain feels so damned strong.
Her always so
loving, so

angry,
holding
tight.

Hugged by the pigs, a fat drunk bellows
in a tongue nobody understands,
his face repulsive, red.

TORCH SONG

Behind a trembling bush,
my best friend raped me,
lit up a flashlight deep inside me.

Asked, in court, to describe
my assailant, I filled
minutes with minute

detail, allowing them, like Bishop
with her fish (which didn't stink?)
to see: his blond hair a haystack

with a needle, his posture
erect, an exclamation,
not a question

mark. Open,
eyes. Breathe,
brain. I want

the world to be our
perfect mother, neither
helping us nor hurting us, simply

holding us, calmly
getting us, eventually,
off. Let us pray

for each pine needle burning
in the sinking sun, needing
in this flaming mouth

to scream.

THE PEDERAST AS PEDAGOGUE

Sunday morning sunlight screams
through yellow curtains of the young
poet's golden-papered bedroom. I,

his mentor, spoon
him, hugging
tightly, un-

able
to just say
no.

His mother, a hooker,
was dragged to Kansas
from Korea, hidden from

the real wife in a tool shed,
raped each night, dead
from suicide two days

after his birth. He, every day,
coaxes me to don the smelly
old overcoat of rabbit pelts

I feel determined to die in, praying
my colleagues will cry I'm a wolf
and fire me free. They're so

fucking sensitive, they're sheep.
When a leaf falls, they'll scamper
off a cliff, invisible, together.

UNDER THE PROJECTION BOOTH

A blond hero's frightened face fills the screen,
the light inside his eyes darting, trying to flee.

Around me, men's bodies stink
of sweat, *soju,* and spicy food.

In a coffin, a tiny TV hangs from pine boards barely
half a foot above his face: he must be buried alive.

On his screen, a bald man in a black suit, hunched
over a desk, laughs through an intercom at his captive.

These bright images fly overhead, inside that tube of light;
floating cigarette smoke makes it seem a roiling river.

A tall boy presses his shoulder against my chest,
gropes around for my zipper, fondles my soft cock.

Inside me, a dry leaf bounces on the stream's surface until
a green leaf rises through the white current, and swims.

"I can turn off your oxygen at any time, you know.
Feel how helpless you are? How weak, in my power?"

I wrap an arm around his waist. Grab at his pants.
He swats my hand away. Speeds up his strokes.

My forehead rubs his neck. My skull
feels like a porch light left on at noon.

The hero's face sweats. His tongue washes his lips.
"Don't even try to speak now," his captor chuckles.

"I can't hear you unless you turn on your mike,
and frankly, my dear, I don't give a damn."

My trick's thin spine digs into this big belly,
the warm skin and the hard bone between us,

our minds, our silent realms, half an inch apart,
me sensing, everywhere, the other's delicacy,

the cascading weight, electric pressure of the self,
his breath, his tongue, heavy inside this mouth.

FROM THE WILDERNESS OF STARS

You who tremble among trees tonight,
listening to black leaves fluttering,
the path behind you
lost, the possibility
of caressing my forehead
keeping you outside, kneeling
in the cracking twigs, holding
up your fingers inside darkness
as if touching the passing wind,

the only holy ghost
is in your mind, a whisper
waiting to come out,
float a few feet off,
enter heaven,
your spent breath.

WITHOUT EXTERNAL REFERENCE

All the village idiot knows how to do, you
know, is fool around.

In his dark, lonesome night,
he feels our orgasms.

If we tug our false
teeth out, kneel

before his bulge,
he will recall

a zoo seal swirling around around
around its tiny tub, rubbing

its belly on the curving
white cement: trans-

fixed, he'll stare
down, tossing

in, why not,
a silver fish,

our tongue.

THE VILLAGE IDIOT DURING
THE RECONSTRUCTION

A red light swings, a train bell
clangs, you all got to stop, but I

stumble out onto the tracks, balance
on a tie, visible, vulnerable. Look

at that 'coon's corpse, its stuck up
paws. Was its soul freed by an angel?

Deep in my dumb brain, the word
emancipation pushes back against

my senses. Piss stinks up the wet
air where, in a dull breeze the flesh

can't hardly feel, the kudzu
tongues flutter, "Wait here. Hug

whatever dark freedom crashes
into your wide-open arms, your trap."

THE VILLAGE IDIOT INSIDE HIS HIDE

The sun pierces fluffy white clouds,
a bullet penetrating a lamb's fleece.

Friendly fire babbling through the black cracked dash,
Earth beckoning, through its thin skin, to the lonely, I

flinch up against the noon-flogged billboard's silver smile
minting personality into this skinny inwardness, famished.

See those tattered panties in the beer-drenched dust?
May I compare them to a boy's shoe filled with blood,

folding ghostly shoulders, trembling
winglessly, into your mind,

my jeans overdyed
red that I might

resemble
kill?

TO THE VILLAGE IDIOT
INSIDE OUR HAUNTED HOUSE

Why not be more positive?
Your shut up mouth is a dead
giveaway you came
from someplace cold.

A pirate bellows, "Dead men tell
no tales," but this dude, he's only
the drama queen who wore green tights
at the Renaissance Faire outside the Wal-Mart.

A psycho thrusts a chainsaw at your fat, passive mask.
Sticking your fist into a tub of noodles,
we snicker. Hear ye? If only
we really could help you slug

your murdered brain
feeling no pain.

THE VILLAGE IDIOT'S OFFENSIVE

Hear him clomp through dry leaves,
white breath haunting his twisted
unkissed lips in lieu of song.

Snub the bugger for grunting,
silently, touchingly, deep
down inside your dumb mind.

Just because he whistles, waves
of baying bitches break through
your brain's gray bedroom,

neglected pets needing
to leap free into the street.
Here sirens shriek.

THE VILLAGE IDIOT AS STOPPED BUCK

Listen to me sing, again,
again, about this self. Don't

you sort of guess I'm blessed
with spoiled credit, spending

free time pigging
out

on in-
tercourse, anonymous, casual?

Why should I eat humble pie instead of ham?
Just because you need to make space in your icebox?

Ain't this hot
bod a plantation,

cut abs, underneath
a tank top gold as corn,

furrows into which
one could spill poisoned seed,

these over-
dyed red jeans, gashed

open around the knees,
curing old meat?

These pea-green boxers need
to be yanked down. Around

my ankles, they'd seem shackles
just like yours, you slave

to love, here in this adult bookstore,
my grin hidden behind the growl of a wild bore,

my eyebeams fencing with each highway robber's
cross-eyed stare, a pair

of owls moaning in the peach
orchard out back, each to each,

me, inside the stench of sweat and cleanser,
some dumb sucker

spackling you, consumer,
paint brush dipped in stripper.

III

INSIDE

SOME FEELING

Slowly, one floats up, the eyes barely
opening, the black night delicately
fading into gray,

the window's rectangle half-visible,
dawn seeming to melt the glass
over the framed photograph of me

as a bald babe. The black lids
close. The mind sleepwalks,
stumbling around inside the brain.

A deep cough, husky with trapped
phlegm. It's my mother, dying,
air scraping her raw.

A box fan grumbles against my bed.
Cool breath hums around my head.
Now comes the pressure of pleasure.

I need some feeling
outside of this dream
one feels alone inside.

The barking starts.
That trapped Doberman reacts
when sunrise flares across the sky.

The neighbor's hungry mutt, then
all our bitches, yowl and howl,
their one voice void of love.

OUR PURSUIT OF HAPPINESS

A blond boy, a homeless hooker, stares
up at our entertainment center. My God,

honey, it's my fault: he seemed
so innocent, twisting at the disco.

He believes we're both outside, changing
oil: therefore, he thinks, he should steal.

I peek through a peephole
in the eye of a giraffe

in a painting mom did
in private as she died.

At a petting zoo, she told me, giraffes
surrounded her, their golden necks bent

down, her palm, covered with Life Savers, out-
stretched, their long tongues flopping across

her lifeline. Their bedroom eyes,
she swore, blinked peacefully.

"I would never let you, lad, be hurt again.
Aren't you missing entertainment, bright

and shiny? You turn around, around,
around, hooked by a power higher

than your will to be alone, stronger
than me, this voice inside you no one hears."

WHAT WE LEFT IN SAN FRANCISCO

1.
Two tourists from Tulsa
trotted from a trolley.

Just under their thin
marble-white skin,

selfish pigs giggled.
I laughed, you attacked,

pinning punk into country,
nailing soul into body,

stabbing in the shoulder
with this here war feather

the outsider of whatever
gender readers prefer

to picture.
Fuckers.

2.
On Alcatraz, our laughing
tour group locked us up,

together, in solitary.
They marched away.

Holding my hand,
you tried teaching

me penmanship, guiding
my fingertips enclosing

the red tip
of this Bic,

our paper your warm wrist,
your pulse throbbing softly

up against your brand
new name, Bird Man.

INCEST

1.
Pretty brother, I belly-
flop onto your grave

and I pray,
"Suffocate

under the weight
of this fat life."

2.
in the fireplace of a chimney made
from headstones, yellow daisies

blaze: later
he takes

a pink teacup rose, balances
it behind his ear: in his brain

a naked boy escapes
his embrace, passes

away to a place
beyond shame:

A REAL WORLD ARROGATES SELF-LOVE

The inside of this mausoleum feels so cold.
Trembling before my white marble plot,
a blank plaque hiding my urn,

I burn tender, lending to the dead,
and chant chitchat into the silence
and offer this fat fruit to the frigid floor.

Who will touch my dates, my name?
I swing open the door, this pane
smudged with fingerprints.

Holding a green hose,
a guard waters green grass.
He smiles, nodding good day.

I bow before a peddler in a blue booth, an erect coffin.
Imagine his living end, surrounded by gum and film.
I select a sack of apple chips, hungry

to feel that he feels my care.
A drunk teenager shoves my ribs.
My intended takes my silver coin

and keeps smiling down at his paper,
untouched by my white face
flowing past out here.

I shall linger here
and buy headlines for our two tongues
and try getting involved, chattering

sadly, "I'm a sacrifice,
I'm not a prostitute.
Please eat me free."

HER RENAISSANCE

Her wings wiggling in dark, cold air
around my body in this wheelchair,

aroused coyotes crying
down in my hot fault,

my huge she screaming *guilty
of effeminacy,* my puppet

personality howling for mercy
on my skull's stage, behind

my hands' un-
folded prayer,

this mask ex-
plodes in tears.

*Mother, turn this self-
hate into humbleness.*

Her blue fruit jar,
stuffed with dust,

its lip shining
like thinking,

sparks in bulb light.

SUSTENANCE

1.
I somehow thought the magpie mine
simply because I had admired it

here and there, bobbing on barbed wire
in what was once free sage, landing

in abandoned rice paddies,
their owners undersold,

its feathers black and white and blue,
a screaming bruise.

2.
I thought I had to have
a reed car seat mat: it had,

woven into it, that symbol
of longevity.

I wanted to cut, in the center, a hole
to shove my neck through, folding

that armor over my shoulders, me
a warlord in a brand new breastplate.

3.
Inches away
purred a lady

protecting her baby: its chew-toy,
a Tupperware pie slice container,

a white plastic wedge
shaped like a wing,

could have been called sculpture,
say, "The Dove of Other Floods."

A SYMBOLIC SENSE OF SELF

Inside a silo, under the chute, I play
in this pocket with the gold wheat I

scooped from the oily cement floor.
Cows groan in sweet-smelling grass.

Overseas, paddies can't
keep up, sucking abuse.

All the forests, all the deer
cleared away, advancing

cannon fodder swore Your angel rose
over the trenches, an image for hope.

Just let one live
the way a baby

must, un-
able to win

what one deserves,
involved, helpless.

Build this body up,
Lord, into a statue

adorned with fresh swan shit
at the edge of a green pond.

DISPLACED PERSON

In the park behind the battlements where my men's group meets,
this body rests, a thing of blood. Mosquitoes murmur in the ears.

A homosexual hippie, a blind boy in his mind massaging him,
    praying
to art, its message psychology, essentially, got bludgeoned
    in the john.

A handsome Israeli soldier passes his pipe. In the lungs, smoke
paints patience paisley, weighs down all these legs. "Combat,"

he says. "It's like being a mad dog. You're not yourself." I want
    to say
I have wounds I could show you in private, but one must listen
    to others.

I'd tug from his headband a loose thread, but that would be
    mere metaphor,
red meat ripped off bone. The whole world felt the pain in
    Hitler's mouth.

     ❧

Thanks, America, for nothing, a quiet day, a plaster Santa, toppled
from some strip mall department store roof, shattered, its empty

face caved in, a crushed cardinal chick's thin, leathery legs
twisted, the dark flesh of its two closed eyelids puffy, soft.

Mourning doves, hiding in my brain's gray leaves, booing,
my bowed head feels heavy, a big bust. Relationships lack

depth: a helicopter appears to be circling among starlings,
a quartet plays for quarters in a tavern by the mosque.

In a meadow, a girl giggles, gluing sequins onto her
clay baby, fixing man. I believe I stink like a burrito.

A HISTORY OF THE ONLY WAR

At battlefields, I need to feel
     alone, free
from my reenacting friends,
     into the dusk-dark, leafy
everlasting
     wound,
to taste, outside this
     flinch-filled air,
the warm salty bone of my own thumb,
     to grasp a gun,
to make it shoot
     me in the mouth,
let freedom ring,
     echoes of screams
floating closer
     through those white
petals exploding,
     through the limbs of dogwood trees,
every way at once
     away from me.

SUNLIGHT AS SWORD

The Golden Horde advanced across the steppes.
Tacked to a tree, a triangular red banner. Boys

who stepped close to the dust clouds always got
brained. Rumors of the world's death crept west.

Astonishing, the damage: sculptures shattered,
paintings slashed, bits of *Piss Christ* scattered.

Teargas hung so thickly it ignited our eyes,
burning the nostrils, the tongue in the mouth

unable to slide this window open,
stick out senseless knowledge

into the present   to be be-
headed, first falling leaf,

that foreign city smelling
delicate in the bright rain.

ABROAD

1.
Jacked someone's dad
in the Gongora Theater.

Drag queens did rancheras,
mocked Mexican whores.

A big-titted Cuban bartender
pounded mint into a tumbler,

flexed her biceps, laughed
that this was Chinese drudgery.

"Are you a romantic? No? Yes,
it's too expensive, I think so."

Sang at my fan, thumping
blade bouncing

breath back down my throat, vibrato
Liza, Judy.

2.
Nothing bad has happened to me
personally for being gay, a rusty

unicycle wobbling
down the wet

bright beach, *Sinfonia*
Concertante seeming to soar down through white clouds
        painted pink by the sunrise, voices

of the violin and the viola so close, best friends touching
in some bowling alley bathroom, laughing

their heads off, running
from security, slimy

serpents sliding back and forth inside two
fists, each inner governor corrupt, too

into it, performing an act, fondling
his microphone, singing flamenco.

THE MATTER

Taxpayers, draftees, the music in our heads sounds good
enough, a bumping book bag slung around his shoulders.

On a yellow legal pad, he jots
while the string quartet jittles:

ponds pop with the o-
mouths of starved carp;

sad Hispanics fish illegally,
their lines jerked delicately;

he'll have to let his sick muscles die, go home.
Even cigarette smoke fails to cling to shirts forever.

Pretty pure white pear tree petals, fallen, cannot cover
the body of that squirrel curled in the gutter.

During Lupercalia, priests in wolfskins,
goading Rome's small populace to re-

produce, dipped feeder mice in gesso,
flung victims against canvas again, again, o heavens

yes. He do believe
the sun is the hot tip

of a bright red penis-shaped gag candle (blow it
out, we can't) atop our wedding cake of clouds.

TWO ROMANCES

1. *Values*

At the airport, laughing kids hop out. Pointing
into cloudy blues, the boys trace each jet drifting
down, seemingly slowly. Parked in pickups, dads
pray for the gazes of gay guys to grace their gazes.

Poised at the asphalt's edge, some stud turns ass
against a Rambler, snubbing a fat troll slumped
over his steering wheel in heart attack or sleep.
Waiting in her station wagon, one wife frowns.

She knows everything. After picking up the mail,
her man picks up males. Her bowed head shades
her lap. "He keeps trying to please me, to fit in."
She forgives whomever stole their wedding gifts,

kissing her watercolor of fire ants swarming
around in an orchid blossom, purple, plastic.

2. *Freedom*

He rolls down the window of his Sonata to hear
moonlight, fireflies orbiting, bullfrogs chortling
in the sluggishly brown stream; a music lover,
sound is magma swelling up his veins, welling

in bright, wet eyes, igniting his cigar, its glowing
tip smelling of toast, his feeling a flame dancing
at the core of a bunch of blackened, rootless roses,
the brain's soft flora in which Beethoven grows.

He plays his own heart's funeral march, waving
his hands over hosta, conducting, praying, thrust
my form, gender puppet, deeper. Make it hump
a green bonfire, hibernating, returning, dying,

invisible,
alone.

REQUIEM

Here at this condemned Pick-n-Save,
its picture windows cracked, streaked

with bird shit or white paint, flesh-
beige tape, dried by the sun, peeling

back, my dying mother bought stacks
of cheap dishes an earthquake shattered.

Amid glass, pack rat crap, horded headlines,
she slowly fell asleep, her body withered

by neglected diabetes, me coming back late
from the sex club, her bathrobe open, ex-

posing her belly, those black, curling hairs.
Far away within the dashboard, woodwinds

fade into the brass, a sort of understated
complicated pain, the body un-

important, impotent, urban
planners having decided

to rip all of this down. The sky seems
the same gray as the parking lot. That QuikFix

on the corner probably pulls in a few thousand
victims, at least, every week. My dope dealer,

a friendly, diabetic single mom, polishes
her station wagon, white suds spurting

from the sponge inside her fist.
Her windshield glitters, sun-

light trapped in tears. No-
thing can be felt, alone.

TCHAIKOVSKY AS THE WATER OF WINTER

I hear the shriek of a tiny pewter stallion, soldered to a bronze ashtray,
dissolving in that dishwasher where all soft metals melt. I try crying.

I see myself bashing my brain free against your picture window,
wanting to sniff, beyond my boundaries, orange-tinted smog.

I scratch your other, murdered son's name in the stucco, and I remember
your dream: he came back home a wounded deer. Terrified, he smeared

blood all over the white walls, those surfaces you once used as a screen,
a girl in pearls and a black dress waving, the roses in the garden bowing

their pink heads. Your gay husband's fingers snaked, in silhouette, across
your face, his nails ripping your cheeks, shredding your aura's red petals.

The adagio lamentoso movement of the Pathetique is your beat softly
slowing down, down, one note murmuring in the basses, cellos, gone.

Pressing my face into damp grass, smelling your grave, I hear you weep,
your boy, stabbed by a boy raped by his own father, tossed into a deep

canyon. There is no snow in California. The ground's way too
hot. In Carolina, I see tears form around twigs, the blossom buds

frozen. Ice ignites the nerves inside this skin. I feel wet, cold
flakes fall lazily from a white sky. I show another family film,

my brother and I dumping snow, sugar, nutmeg, Kool Whip
into your green bowl, then spooning our ice cream into you.

AT SAINT MARTIN-IN-THE-FIELDS

A heaven-blue oval of stained glass glows
opaquely, reflecting tiny, trembling flames.

The torment in mother's eyes washed away
from family memory, personality, finally,

history, empty, body ready
to curl alone around death,

I cry on worn-down marble steps. Dignity
and a dress shirt make one sit up. Endlessly

held days have burned into the fingers traces
of warmth that should be pressed into playing

tight strings. The ghosts inside music mosey
slowly past, crumbling, reforming, moving

forever forward into the breath
of the living, the having lived.

AFTERWORD

If Christopher Davis were a painter his poems might look like the work of Francis Bacon, with gouge marks in the canvas. In syntax often fractured, or blown apart entire by the poems' jet-fuel mixture of eros and thanatos, *A History of the Only War* gives us the gorgeous/terrifying language of an exploration that is at once sexual and spiritual, bodily and linguistic.

As I read it, the Only War is the one fought inside each of us, the one that precedes all other wars, whether interpersonal or international. With this view Davis takes his place in a long line of mystical poets, those particularly for whom the body is the ultimate battleground for the soul. Though his ancestry can be traced to Hopkins, those expecting a version of Hopkins are in for a shock: Davis is completely and irrevocably of his time—a twenty-first century American poet, with all the connotations that come trailing that indeterminate title.

One could also call Christopher Davis the best of a small group of poets practicing a quickened form of contemporary Expressionism. Though they touch down often in a recognizable American landscape, his poems are far more interested in a kind of Roethkean journey to the interior than in the rendering of outer reality. Davis generally begins with a narrative, more or less explicit, often detailing a furtive sexual encounter. But the narrative cannot hold, and the scene shifts, sideways, to a new locale, with new and tentatively related actors. Then at some point the entire ground of narrative gives way, and we are given a flurry of wild images, simultaneously beautiful and despairing. It is sometimes as if a scene in a film noir were suddenly interrupted by the swooping arrival of a Crayola bright jungle parrot . . .

I find the visionary passion of Davis' work brave and exciting. The fierce, searing beauty of its sound and sense is astringent tonic to paler versions of what passes for poetry. *A History of the Only War* is a heartbreaking conflation of sex, death, and the divine. But it is not some postmodern parody—this is *personal*. And Davis means every word.

—Jeffery Skinner

Christopher Davis is the author of *The Tyrant of the Past and the Slave of the Future*, which received the 1988 Associated Writing Programs Poetry Award, and *The Patriot*, which appeared in 1998 in the University of Georgia Press Contemporary Poetry Series. His poems have appeared in many journals, including *American Poetry Review, Black Warrior Review, Colorado Review, Denver Quarterly, Fence, Harvard Review*, and *The Journal* and in several anthologies. Born in Los Angeles, he received an MFA from the Iowa Writer's Workshop in 1985, and is now an associate professor of creative writing at the University of North Carolina at Charlotte.